Dear God Kids

Annie Fitzgerald

EBURY PRESS

Published by Ebury Press
National Magazine House
72 Broadwick Street
London W1V 2BP

First Impression 1985

Illustrations and text by Anne Fitzgerald

ISBN 0 85223 482 1

Printed and bound in Great Britain by
Butler & Tanner Ltd, Frome and London

Dear God Kids®

Dear God,
- are you watching?

2-13

Dear God Kids®

Dear God,
.....That's it for tonight
....but I'll have more
tomorrow.
G'night!

Annie

2-14

© 1984 INTERCONTINENTAL GREETINGS LTD. DIST. KING FEATURES SYNDICATE

Dear God Kids®

Dear God,
- I want to send
you a present
...... but I don't know
your address

Annie

2-16

Dear God Kids®

Dear God,
- You know all
The answers.... Right?
...Could you give me a little
hint?

Annie

2-17

Dear God Kids®

Dear God,
..... maybe a
little push - huh?

Annie

2-18

DEAR GOD KIDS®

DEAR GOD,

......AND I NEED ALL THIS STUFF REAL SOON! .. I'LL WORK ON ANOTHER LIST TOMORROW

Annie

2-20

DEAR GOD KIDS®

DEAR GOD,

- YOUR MOVE!

Annie

2-21

Dear God Kids®

Dear God,
- If I forget you
...... please don't forget me

2-23

Dear God Kids®

Dear God,
..... Oh! -
I've just been
thinking how
good you are
to me -
Thanks!

Annie

2-24

Dear God Kids®

Dear God,

..... I BET YOU LOVE DOGS TOO!

Annie

2-28

DEAR GOD KIDS®

DEAR GOD,

...CAN YOU GET THIS CHANNEL IN HEAVEN?

Annie

3-2

DEAR GOD KIDS®

DEAR GOD,

WOW! ..... HAVE YOU READ THE NEWSPAPER TODAY?

Annie

3-3

Dear God Kids.

Dear God,
....are you ever
depressed?

Annie

3-5

Dear God Kids®

Dear God,

.....sure hope you're wearing your raincoat!

Annie

3-8

Dear God Kids®

Dear God,
- Do you like naughty kids too?

Annie

3-10

Dear God Kids®

Dear God,
...what are you wearing in Heaven this year?

3-12

Dear God Kids®

Dear God,

...When I take a nap you watch out for me... right?

When do you take your nap?

...Annie

3-13

Dear God Kids®

Dear God,

....Must rush

... Don't want to miss the bus

3-15

Dear God Kids®

Dear God,

... What do you use for bait?

3-1

Annie

Dear God Kids.

Dear God,

... Do the angels have to eat all their spinach, too?

3-19

Dear God Kids.

Dear God,

.... If you write another book .... can I be in it?

Annie

3-21

©1984 INTERCONTINENTAL GREETINGS LTD. DIST.: KING FEATURES SYNDICATE

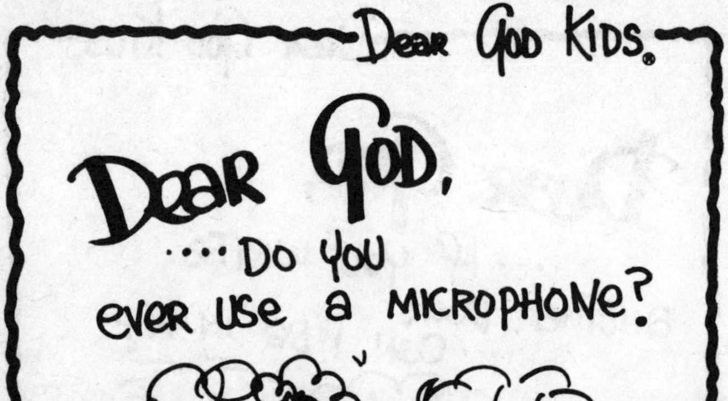

Dear God Kids®

Dear God,

.... Do you ever use a microphone?

Annie

3-22

Dear God Kids®

Dear God,

..... I'm getting there

3-23

Annie

Dear God Kids®

Dear God,

.... We had such an exciting day

..... Did you see everything?

Annie

3-26

Dear God Kids®

Dear God,

- You know, I think that caterpillar is limping on one leg

Annie 3-27

Dear God Kids®

Dear God,

....Just how did you do it?

Annie

3-28

Dear God Kids®

Dear God,

- Do you ever run out of stories?

3-30

Dear God Kids®

Dear God,
—.... and mom says
that you can talk to
everybody in the whole
world...
imagine?

...Annie

3-31

Dear God Kids®

Dear God,
—What is
the name of your
airline?...

Annie

4-2

Dear God Kids®

Dear God,
- If I be quiet....
.....Can I hear your voice?

Annie 4-3

Dear God Kids®

Dear God,
....Scouts honor,
I'll be good!

Annie 4-4

© 1984 INTERCONTINENTAL GREETINGS LTD. DIST. KING FEATURES SYNDICATE

DEAR GOD KIDS®

DEAR GOD,
IT'S ME
AGAIN...

Annie

4-5

DEAR GOD KIDS®

DEAR GOD,
– CAN YOU SPEAK
MY LANGUAGE?

– Annie

4-6

© 1984 INTERCONTINENTAL GREETINGS LTD. DIST. KING FEATURES SYNDICATE

DEAR GOD KIDS®

Dear GOD,
- If I TURN away
from you
..... please DON'T TURN
away from me

Annie

4-7

DEAR GOD KIDS®

Dear GOD,
How's THAT?

Annie

4-9

DEAR GOD KIDS®

Dear God,

– That was easy

..... You must have been concentrating

Annie

4-10

DEAR GOD KIDS®

Dear God,

.... was that a message from you?

Annie

4-12

Dear God KIDS®

DEAR GOD,

.... YOU KNOW ITS
aMaZING, TO THINK THAT YOU
KNOW EVERYTHING
aBOUT
EVERYBODY!

4-16 Annie

DEAR GOD KIDS®

DEAR GOD,

....WHEN YOU WERE LITTLE ...WHO READ STORIES TO YOU?

Annie 4-17

DEAR GOD KIDS®

DEAR GOD,

.... LET'S TAKE a BREAK

Annie 4-18

DEAR GOD KIDS®

DEAR GOD,

.... DID YOU EVER THINK YOU'D LIKE TO BE ALONE ..... AND THEN WHEN YOU ARE ALONE .. YOU DON'T LIKE IT?

♡ Annie

4-19

DEAR GOD KIDS®

DEAR GOD,

.... NOW DON'T FORGET ..... MY CAT LIKES A SPECIAL BRAND OF CAT FOOD

♡ Annie

4-20

DEAR GOD KIDS®

DEAR GOD,
... YOU CAN HELP TO PUSH IT IF YOU LIKE

Annie
4-21

DEAR GOD KIDS®

DEAR GOD,
... I WISH WE COULD SEE YOU ON TELEVISION

4-23

Dear God Kids®

Dear God,

...If you get Dad to raise my allowance ....I'LL SPLIT IT WITH YA, OK?

4-25

Annie

Dear God Kids®

Dear God,

....Do you tell the sea when to stop on the shore?

Annie 4-27

Dear God Kids®

Dear God,

....Do you have to change the batteries in the stars?

Annie 5-2

DEAR GOD KIDS®

DEAR GOD,

...any SUGGESTIONS?

5-5

Annie

Dear God Kids®

Dear God,

...You know some of this news could be depressing ..... if you weren't in control

Annie 5-8

Dear God Kids®

Dear God,

....Before you do another thing..... would you check out my day before I get going?

5-9 Annie

©1984 INTERCONTINENTAL GREETINGS LTD. DIST.: KING FEATURES SYNDICATE

Dear God Kids®

Dear God,

.....I'm waiting for your call

5-11

Annie...

Dear God Kids®

Dear God,

there ......what do you think?

Annie 5-14

Dear God Kids®

DEAR GOD,

.... I HOPE YOU DON'T CATCH MY COLD

Annie

5-16

Dear God Kids®

DEAR GOD,

...DO STARS EVER CRASH INTO ONE ANOTHER, LIKE US SOME-TIMES?

5-17

Annie

©1984 INTERCONTINENTAL GREETINGS LTD. DIST.: KING FEATURES SYNDICATE

Dear God Kids®

Dear God,

.... If you are doing nothing...... Would you like to play with us?

Dear God Kids®

Dear God,

...Do you know where I am when I don't?

5-19

Annie

Dear God Kids®

Dear God,

....are you up?

5-24

Annie

DEAR GOD KIDS.

DEAR GOD,

....DO YOU KNOW THAT I'M ON A DIET?

DEAR GOD KIDS.

DEAR GOD,

....IMAGINE, THE SUN IS HANGING UP THERE

....AND I'M SITTING DOWN HERE

5-26

Annie

DEAR GOD KIDS®

DEAR GOD,

... WHEN IT SNOWS
... IS IT AN OVERFLOW FROM HEAVEN?

5-28 Annie

DEAR GOD KIDS®

DEAR GOD,

TELL THAT TREE
TO GIVE MY KITE
BACK

5-31 Annie

Dear God Kids®

Dear God,

.....I suppose
You trained
him to do that

6-2

Annie

Dear God Kids®

Dear God,
I'm not saying I don't like peas ..... I just don't like them that much

6-4 Annie

Dear God Kids®

Dear God,
... Did you ever have one of those "days?"

Annie 6-5

Dear God Kids®

Dear God,

....If you're not too busy would you look over this? Thanks!

6-7 Annie

Dear God Kids®

Dear God,

....Just how do you do it.... put all that salt in the sea?

6-8 Annie

Dear God Kids®

Dear God,

.... I'm knitting my brother socks .... but don't let him grow any more until I'm finished

6-11

Annie

Dear God Kids®

Dear God,

.... I just can't sleep

.... want to talk for a while?

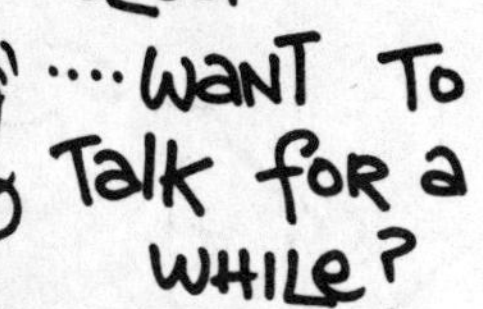

Annie

6-12

Dear God Kids®

Dear God,

.... I just can't find your place on the map

Annie

6-13

Dear God Kids®

Dear God,

....Boy!

You sure did turn up the thermometer today!

6-14

....Annie

Dear God Kids®

Dear God,

....whatever you do don't take a day off tomorrow ....I've got a test

Annie 6-15

DEAR GOD KIDS®

DEAR GOD,

.... DO YOU STILL HAVE TO DO YOUR HOMEWORK?

DEAR GOD KIDS®

DEAR GOD,

.... I'M GETTING CLOSER .... HUH?

6-18

Annie

Dear God Kids®

Dear God,

...Do you ever get mad at anybody?

6-20

Annie

Dear God Kids®

Dear God,

....If I do the skipping ....will you do the counting?

Annie 6-21

Dear God Kids®

Dear God,

....Do the angels hitch-hike on your clouds?

6-22 Annie

Dear God Kids®

Dear God,

...You sure tell some stories

6-27

Annie

Dear God Kids®

Dear God,

...You must have made laughing ...It's so good

6-28

Annie

Dear God Kids®

Dear God,

....and you can give them chicken pox ....back to the chickens

Annie

6-29

DEAR GOD KIDS®

DEAR GOD,

MOM SAYS I'M GROWING LIKE A WEED ...DID YOU MAYBE FERTILIZE ME TOO MUCH?

7-3

Annie

Dear God Kids®

Dear God,

Do you ever have to say good bye to anybody?

7-5

Annie

Dear God Kids®

Dear God,

...This is for you ...I'm guessing your measurements

7-6

Annie

Dear God Kids®

Dear God,

... How about
That?

G
O
D

7-9

Annie

Dear God Kids®

Dear God,

....Do you have enough mountains for everyplace?

7-10

Annie

DEAR GOD KIDS®

DEAR GOD,

...DO YOU GET VACATIONS TOO?

Annie

7-12

DEAR GOD KIDS®

DEAR GOD,

...IT'S CHECKING IN TIME .... DO I HAVE TO GO?

FLY

7-13

Annie

Dear God Kids®

DEAR GOD,

..Here Comes SUMMeR

...GOOD BYe WINTeR

7-16

Annie

Dear God Kids®

Dear God,

...I just love pizza..

Want some?

Annie

7-18

Dear God Kids®

Dear God,

OK... I'M ready to start again

Annie 7-19

Dear God Kids®

Dear God,

... IT'S all worked out... the route for our vacation ... coming?

Annie 7-21

Dear God Kids®

Dear God,

...all men are equal... How come some of us weigh more?

7-24

Annie

Dear God Kids®

Dear God,
...You must
have had one
all
along

7-27

Annie

Dear God Kids®

Dear God,

...Is that a message?

...Tell him to wait for an answer

Annie

7-28

Dear God Kids®

Dear God,

...Do you know that my teacher is the best in the world?

7-30

Annie

Dear God Kids®

Dear God,

...OK I'm ready.... Now you send the customers

8-3

Annie

Dear God Kids®

Dear God,
...I'm sending this express .... so would you return it express?

EXPRESS MAIL

Annie 8-4

Dear God Kids®

Dear God,
... Do you have discount stores in heaven?

8-6

Annie

Dear God Kids®

Dear God,

...YOU WIN SOME
... YOU LOSE SOME

8-8

Annie

Dear God Kids®

Dear God,

I just love livin'

8-9 Annie

Dear God Kids®

Dear God,

There's always enough to share... right?

8-10 Annie

Dear God Kids®

Dear God,

... I'm getting there

Annie

8-11

Dear God Kids®

Dear God,

... He is slow

.... But

He can't

Help

it

Annie

8-14

Dear God Kids®

Dear God,

Need a

trumpet player?

8-15

Annie

Dear God Kids®

Dear God,

... You've got a LOT of KIDS

Annie

8-17

Dear God Kids®

Dear God,

...I sure hope you'll be here for my finals..
.... but you will.
...right?

Annie

8-18

Dear God Kids®

Dear God,

... I just love surprises ...Have you some for today?

Annie

8-24

Dear God Kids®

Dear God,

...You did a fine job

8-28

Annie

DEAR GOD KIDS®

DEAR GOD,

...HEY!

DO ANGELS HAVE PEN-PALS?

Annie

8-30

DEAR GOD KIDS®

DEAR GOD,

THAT'S IT.

....NOW I'M WAITING TO HEAR FROM YOU

Annie

9-1

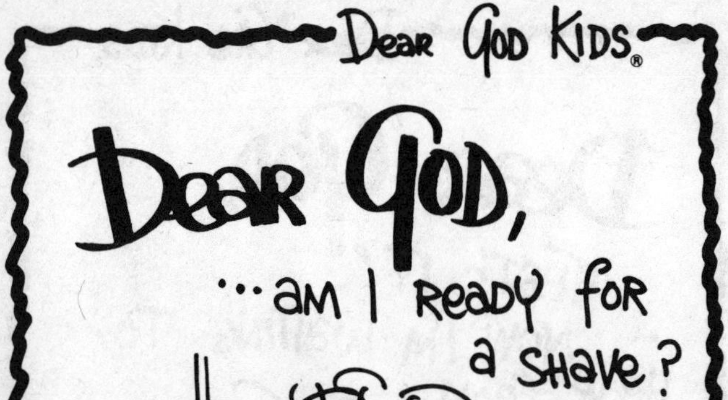

Dear God Kids®

Dear God,

...am I ready for a shave? ...a little one ..... maybe ..huh?

Annie

9-3

Dear God Kids®

Dear God,

...Let's go for gold!

9-5

Annie

Dear God Kids®

Dear God,

... Boy!
I could do with wings too

Annie

9-7

Dear God Kids®

Dear God,

.... Hey!
Did you know that you can cook out of a book?

Annie

9-8

©1984 INTERCONTINENTAL GREETINGS LTD. DIST. KING FEATURES SYNDICATE

Dear God Kids®

Dear God,

... You've got so many kids I thought I'd better send you a special photograph of me

Annie

9-11

Dear God Kids®

Dear God,

...You can pick it up anytime you like

Dear God Kids®

Dear God,

...I'll be glad when this cleaning up business is all over

9-13

Annie

Dear God Kids®

Dear God,

.. Do you have
a place of your own
... to get away from it all?

Annie

9-15

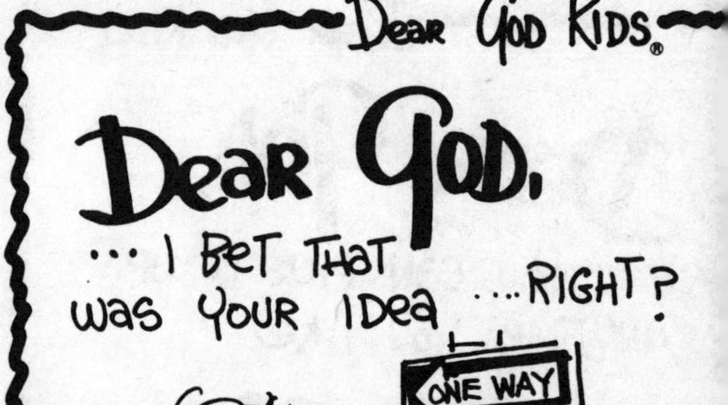

Dear God Kids®

Dear God,

... I bet that
was your idea .... right?

ONE WAY

9-17

... Annie

Dear God Kids®

Dear God,

... what a decision

.... should I bring my lunch ...or buy it?

9-20 Annie

DEAR GOD KIDS®

DEAR GOD,

...THIS ONE IS especially FOR YOU

Annie

9-21

Dear God Kids®

Dear God,

...Thanks for tuning in

9-27

Annie

Dear God Kids®

DEAR GOD,

...YeaH! I GUESS YOU MUST HAVE TRAFFIC LIGHTS IN HEAVEN

Annie

9-28

Dear God Kids®

DEAR GOD,

...WE MAY BE TWINS .... BUT WE'VE GOT OUR VERY OWN MINDS

9-29